I0190242

He Is Risen Indeed!

Gurden Henley

C.S.S. Publishing Company, Inc.
Lima, Ohio

HE IS RISEN INDEED!

Copyright © 1986 by
The C.S.S. Publishing Company, Inc.
Lima, Ohio

YOU MAY, BY THE PURCHASE OF THESE C.S.S. DRAMAS, MAKE AS MANY
COPIES AS YOU NEED (by any means, electronic or mechanical, including photocopy-
ing) in order to stage a performance of these plays. No additional royalty or performing fee is required. Inquiries may be addressed to: C.S.S. Publishing Company, Inc.,
628 South Main Street, Lima, Ohio 45804.

O86 2T

6813 / ISBN 0-89536-795-5   PRINTED IN U.S.A.

Table of Contents

1. Sunrise Surprise 5
   A drama for five participants

2. A Zealot's Greatest Battle 15
   A drama for eight participants

3. When Old Nick Met Nicodemus 29
   A drama for ten participants plus extras

Author's Introduction

It was twenty-five years ago, when I was a fledgling pastor, that I was first introduced to the effectiveness of drama in the Christian worship service. A young lady who was new to our congregation had been very active in high school and college drama, and wanted to do something for Christmas that year in the way of a play. Not a musical . . . not a pageant . . . but a drama.

She gave me a simple play script to read. I was not overly impressed with the play, but thought it sounded a bit interesting, and even consented to be one of the members of the cast. The play went off without a hitch, and I made a great discovery . . . the people talked about the play for weeks after. They examined the experiences in the play, likened them to their own lives, and shared such things as, "you know, how the character in the play reacted is how we, as Christians, should react." I found them talking about and learning from this drama for weeks, when they could hardly remember, from Sunday to Sunday, my best work in sermonizing.

When I saw the effectiveness of drama, I began searching for other plays . . . good plays with "heart" that really made you think, made you cry, made you laugh.

I made the sad discovery that most religious plays were tamed down so that the "laugh lines" would only give the audience a sweet smile . . . one that would be fully acceptable on the "holy ground" of a church platform. I also discovered that most religious plays were written extremely carefully not to arouse too much emotion. We wanted tears in our eyes when we went to a theatre or movie, but not at church. Becoming disgusted with the watered-down versions of religious drama, I began writing my own plays and directing them. Folks in the area soon learned that when we performed a play, it would be fun, interesting, and would have "heart." The crowds came. We had repeat performances, toured with the plays, performed them on television, and turned away hundreds of people from our church that seats 1100, on the nights when the plays were presented.

Then, the "mini-play" was born in my heart. These are plays that I use as an appendix to a holiday sermon . . . and these are what this book is all about.

In our church ad on the day before Easter Sunday, I will announce my topic and then mention that following the sermon we will present a sparkling new mini-play, giving the title and listing the cast names.

I have never done this without having the Sanctuary jammed for at least three Sunday morning services, and usually having people unhappily turned away at the doors.

I present this book to you who are busy pastors, and unable to write your own plays. Give it a try. Add a mini-play to your Easter or Lent sermon. Tie it in with your message, and watch your attendance soar . . . and listen to the comments such as, "It made Easter so real to me, it was like really being there!"

G. F. Henley

Sunrise Surprise

Cast (in order of appearance)

NARRATOR
MARY MAGDALENE
JOHN
PETER
JESUS

Production Note

At the beginning, and then at the close, of "Sunrise Surprise," it is suggested that the scene be changed by "revolving the stage." This option is possible in a stage or theatre setting where such mechanics can be attended to. For those planning to present the drama in a chancel setting, the stage setting could be changed by manually moving the props; by the use of lighting; or by suggestion on the part of the actors.

Introduction

I have always had an aversion to using Jesus as one of the characters in any of the many plays I have written and produced. However, in this one, I broke from my policy and it proved to be a warm and refreshing break.

I chose, to portray Jesus, a gentleman from our congregation who had a full beard. We encouraged him not to get a haircut until after the presentation; he did not wear a wig. We bathed him in a warm spotlight, and he did the job beautifully. Of course, at the end of the presentation, you'll see we had him freeze his pose as we revolved him off stage.

Setting: *Early the first Easter morning*

Narrator

Our drama takes place very early in the morning of the first day of the week. Usually, at such a time, the city of Jerusalem is bustling with activity. One normally sees numbers of little donkeys carrying huge loads of vegetables or fruit; and men and women with long sticks, shouting at those donkeys or at each other as they vie for the best spot in the marketplace. But this day it is strangely quiet. There is little show of life in the winding old cobblestone streets of this ancient city. The great festival of the Passover has just ended. Just last evening, following the Sabbath sunset, these same streets had been filled with people. Pipers, drums and tambourines had played the exotic festival music. People danced and partied in these streets, and the wine flowed freely. So, this morning, most of the city is still asleep . . . yet, not all. For a few, it has been a time of great sorrow . . . weeping . . . remembering . . . for the body of one they loved, Jesus of Nazareth, lies cold and dead in a borrowed grave. *(Stage revolves to reveal scene of tomb)* Now, a lone figure makes its way silently through the shadows of the deserted streets. It is one of those who has mourned through this festival . . . it is Mary Magdalene.

Mary

(Talking to herself as she walks to the tomb) A woman should be afraid to be alone in a dark cemetery . . . but I am not afraid! Perhaps it is because I am still too numb from the awful tragedy. Or, perhaps I am not afraid because the body of him whom I love most is here. *(Begins to weep softly)* Body . . . dead . . . It's senseless . . . so

senseless. I was so sure he was the Messiah! *(She sits down)* The other women should be here soon. Peter asked us all to meet here at sunrise so we could give his body proper embalming. *(Weeps again)* I can't stand to think of it! *(Pauses)* I don't know what hurts the most . . . the loss of my friend, or the loss of my hope! *(Looking up)* Oh, Yahweh . . . how could you permit such a thing? I ask you what he asked you from the cross just before he died, "Oh, My God, My God, why did you forsake him"? *(She calms a bit)* My hope . . . gone! *(She gets up, looks toward the tomb)* In there, behind the stone that seals the door, lies the body of him who I thought to be the hope of the world! *(She notices that the stone has been rolled away, and gasps in amazement)* The stone! Someone has rolled it back! Someone has been here! *(She first peeks in . . . then walks in)* He's gone! Someone has stolen the body! Oh, no . . . now they will place him on shameful public display. The Pharisees were so disappointed that he died on the eve of the Sabbath and had to be taken down from the cross so soon so that their Sabbath would not be defiled. Now they will hang him up somewhere . . . probably in the Temple area . . . and hold his body up to mockery for all to see and laugh at. They probably kept that awful sign that said, "King of the Jews." Oh no . . . no . . . *(In thought)* Peter . . . I must tell Peter and John! *(Shouts as she runs out)* Peter! Peter! They have stolen away the body of our Lord!

(All is quiet on stage for a moment . . . then John runs in and peeks into the tomb, but does not enter; then Peter runs up all out of breath)

John
(Very excitedly and out of breath) Peter . . . Mary was right! The stone has been rolled away, and I can't see his

body in there!

Peter

(Rushing into the tomb) Gone! He's gone! Those dirty Pharisees have taken him for further humiliation! (In great anguish) John, I felt I could make up for my denying him by at least standing up for him in death . . . by giving him a proper burial, with a beautiful memorial plaque. It was the least I could do . . . (Begins to weep) But now, even that chance is gone! Gone . . . just like the best friend I ever had. (Weeps harder) Haven't they done enough to humiliate and discredit him?

John

But, Peter . . . (In great thought) Look . . . the grave clothes are all still lying as though the body were in them; except for the linen cloth which covered his face . . . it is all neatly folded up. It's strange . . . if someone stole his body, they wouldn't take the time to fold the linen cloth. And it seems strange that the grave clothes were removed and then re-wrapped as if there were a body in them, and returned to their proper place. You'd think a grave robber would rush right in, grab the body, and run. It's very strange. It's as if the body mysteriously slipped out of the grave clothes. (Pensively) Do you suppose? . . . Do you suppose he came back to life?

Peter

John, you suffer from too much grief! Have you forgotten just how final death is? Remember, we all saw him die. We all saw that Roman spear pierce into his side, mangling of all his vital organs. Had he not been dead, he surely couldn't live with a spear twisting in his heart! And where are the Roman soldiers who were ordered here to guard his tomb? Did they simply leave, when the Pharisees and religious leaders demanded his body? See, their fire is still smoldering!

John
But he *did* say, "If you destroy this temple, in three days I will restore it"! Remember, he pointed to himself when he said it. Perhaps he has mysteriously come back to life. He brought Lazarus back to life . . . and others. Remember the daughter of Jairus? Certainly he could do it to himself! Remember all the miraculous things he did . . . impossible things like walking on the water? Super-human things! I believe he *could* come back to life!

Peter
John, John . . . go home and get some rest! Your body and mind are tired. Your emotions are high, and your imagination is playing tricks on you. *(Mary runs up and Peter speaks to her)* It is as you say, Mary. His body has been stolen! So, now we'll face more persecution and embarrassment as they humiliate him the more!

Mary
(In great anquish) What is to *happen* to us, Peter? What are we to do?

Peter
Well, I don't know about anyone else, but I'm going back to my old occupation . . . I'm going fishing.

Mary
But, Peter, you can't do that! If you do that, what is to happen to the rest of us? I can't go back to my old life! At least, I don't want to go back . . . Peter, remember,

I was a woman of the street! Can you imagine how rotten my life was? On good days I could find myself waking up between the silk sheets of a Roman centurion's bed . . . but on the bad days I slept with the winos in the gutter. And, there were more bad days than good! Then Jesus came . . . he forgave me . . . he believed in me . . . he gave me another chance. He changed me! I can't go back to that! *(Very urgently)* Peter, you're the leader! If you desert his philosophies, then everything he lived and taught will be lost. You're the leader, and if *you* forsake his cause, all the rest of us will also fail!

Peter
(Taking Mary's face in his hands) Mary, you're dead wrong! I'm not the leader! I'm the failure of the group. If I had the nerve of Judas, I'd probably do away with myself as he did. I'm a failure, and the only thing I know to do is go back to my old occupation. *(To John)* Now, let's go home and get some rest. We're going to need it for the days ahead.

Mary
I want to stay here in the Garden for awhile. The other women are coming with the embalming spices. I'll wait for them, and tell them the sad news.

John
But wait a minute, Peter, I just remembered something else that Jesus said one time. Remember, he said, "As Jonah was three days in the belly of the fish, so must the Son of Man be three days in the heart of the earth." He could have meant he would be dead for three days. Remember the parable about the grain of corn?

Peter

(Interrupting) Come on, John . . . you're very tired.

John

(As they slowly depart) Remember, the corn had to be planted in the earth and die if it was to come into newness of life. That's what he said. Peter . . . don't you remember? And he also said . . . (John's voice fades out as they disappear out of sight)

(Mary sits down on a rock, places her face in her hands, and weeps softly. Jesus walks up behind her)

Jesus

Why are you weeping?

Mary

(Not looking up nor around) Because they have stolen away the body of my Lord. You must be the gardener . . . if you know where they have taken him, please tell me so I can go to him.

Jesus

(With great expression) Mary . . . Mary

Mary

(Upon recognizing his voice, her head lifts slowly and she turns around slowly; with great expression, her mouth falls open and her eyes light up in astonishment) Master! Master . . . it's You! (She falls face down at his feet)

Jesus

Yes, Mary, it is I. But, please do not touch me as yet, for

I have not yet ascended to my Father. Mary . . . *(She looks up at him)*I need you to do something for me.

Mary
Yes, Master . . . anything you ask.

Jesus
I need for you to quickly go to my disciples and tell them that I rose from the dead.

Mary
Yes, Master. You're alive! It's too wonderful to be true!

Jesus
Quickly, Mary . . . please do as I say. Tell my disciples that I am alive. And, Mary: Peter is hurting so much . . . be sure to tell Peter! *(Motions for her to be going)*

Mary
(Backing slowly away) You're alive! You're alive!

Jesus
Be sure to tell Peter!

Mary
(She begins to run, a few steps at a time, looking back from time to time. She shouts as she goes) PETER! JOHN! He's alive! JESUS IS ALIVE! Peter . . . he told me to tell you . . . *(Stage revolves with Jesus standing on it, frozen in a position with his arms outstretched in a welcoming manner)*

A Zealot's Greatest Battle

Cast (in order of appearance)

MATTHEW
BARABBAS
SIMON
ANNA
JAMES THE LESS
PHILIP
JUDAS, NOT ISCARIOT
ANDREW

Introduction

If one is to get a true picture of the great conflict that went on in the mind of Simon the Zealot, one needs to consider his background. Perhaps a paragraph could be included in the program that would establish Simon's ties with the Zealottes and his hatred of Rome. Care should be taken that the paragraph not be too long, or the interest of the readers will be lost.

Scene: *Three crosses on Golgotha, in dawn's light on the first Easter morning. Lighting gets gradually brighter as story unfolds.*

Matthew

(Walking onto dimly lit stage, grimaces as he looks at center cross) When you are up close, it seems so much bigger. *(Looks away)* I can't bear to look at it! The Romans have certainly been successful in propagating fear through the use of this torturous death instrument. *(Sits down)* I wonder . . . could that be one of the reasons that I, at one time, sided in with Rome . . . fear? *(Looks up at cross)* This will be the third day since he hung there. Only three days . . . but how I miss him! The best friend I ever had! *(Begins to weep)* He loved me in spite of my sins. He accepted me! *(Weeps quietly for a few moments)*

Barabbas

(Slips in silently; stands looking at Matthew who is sitting beneath the cross, weeping) *(A bit sarcastically)* You are aware that it is unbecoming for a man to weep?

Matthew

(Who is startled, and stutters a bit) Uh . . . uh . . . I believed I was alone. Forgive me.

Barabbas

You're a friend or relative, I presume?

Matthew

He was my friend. I came here to be alone with my memories.

Barabbas
I came here because I wanted to see the place where I should have died.

Matthew
Where *you* should have died? Oh. I see. Then you must be . . . Barabbas.

Barabbas
"Lucky Barabbas," they call me. *(Looks at cross)* These are gruesome-looking things up close! For months now, in my dreams, I have died on that cross. The nightmares started as soon as I knew I had received the death sentence. Oh, yes . . . I laughed and cursed on the outside . . . but on the inside, I trembled: But now look at me . . . *(Laughs)* Lucky Barabbas! That's me, Lucky Barabbas! When the scarlet uniformed soldiers came to get me to be crucified, I couldn't believe it . . . "You're free!" they said. What an exhilarating moment! All the other inmates couldn't believe it, either. They were all shouting "good-bye" to me . . . Lucky Barabbas! *(Moves closer and peers into Matthew's face)* Say . . . don't I know you from somewhere?

Matthew
It is possible that you might have seen me traveling with Jesus. My name is Matthew, and I've been one of his disciples these past three years.

Barabbas
Matthew? No, that doesn't ring a bell at all. But, then, I've been incarcerated for the past few years, so I wouldn't have had a chance to see you with Jesus. *(Peering closely into his face)* But, I know you, I'm sure of it! Capernaum? Have

you ever been there?

Matthew

Capernaum is my home town. I lived there up until three years ago when I began traveling with Jesus.

Barabbas

I thought so, I know you from Capernaum . . . *(Very loudly)* I've got it . . . Levi! You are that traitor tax collector, Levi! *(He is up in a flash; has startled Matthew and wrestled him to the ground. He takes out his sica, holds it to Matthew's throat)* That lousy Publican tax collector, Levi! I knew I remembered you from somewhere! Lucky Barabbas . . . free for only three days, and already fate has put at the tip of my dagger one of my sworn enemies!

Matthew

I told you, I am Matthew! I am no longer Levi! You're right: he was a cheat and a crook . . . but Jesus changed all of that! Jesus gave. . .

Barabbas

(Not even listening to him) Levi! . . . Is this my lucky day!

Matthew

(Continues while Barabbas speaks) Jesus gave me a new life and a new name. The old Levi made restitution for everything he took dishonestly.

Barabbas

(Still not hearing him) How well I do remember you, with your Roman bodyguards. But I knew if I waited long enough I would catch you without them. *(Presses sica into his throat)* I'll slit your throat from ear to ear. I'll cut out

your heart and have it presented to your lofty Roman over-
seer. What do you have to say to that?

Matthew

I'm not afraid to die, Barabbas! Now, with Jesus dead, I
could almost welcome death. If you cut my heart out —
and I have no doubt that you will — Put your ear close
to my chest. With my last heart's beat it will be saying, "I
love you, Barabbas"! I, who once hated Zealots, through
the power of Christ's love will say, "I love you!"

Barabbas

(Becoming very angry) Your doubletalk is going to get you
nowhere. I'll be honest with you: *I hate you!* I hate all Pub-
licans! I hate all Romans! *(Moves back his sica, as if to strike)*
Better blood than yours has stained the blade of this sica!

Simon

(Who has crept up; he wrests the sica away from Barabbas' hand) Barabbas! You were about to kill my friend,
Matthew!

Barabbas

Simon! . . . Simon the Zealot! *(They embrace)*

Simon

Barabbas, it's been years since I've seen you!

Barabbas

And I you, Simon! But I've been out of circulation for a
good while! It's so good to see my most promising young
officer again!

Simon

And it's good to see my old captain once more. *(Motions to Matthew, who still half lies on the ground)* Looks like you're still up to your old tricks . . . you almost did in one of my best friends, Matthew!

Barabbas

Matthew? I mistook him for Levi, the dirty traitor of Capernaum. They are dead ringers for each other!

Simon

The traitor, Levi, died three years ago. This is the born-again Matthew!

Barabbas

(A bit confused) Well, they sure look alike!

Simon

Matthew, I'm glad I found you. Your younger brother, James, is looking for you. He really needs you . . . he is so despondent since the death of Jesus!

Matthew

Thanks, Simon . . . I'll go to him at once. Nice to meet you, Barabbas.

Barabbas

And you, too, Matthew. Sorry I mistook you for a tax collector . . . what an insult! But, you want to know something ironic? Remember, Simon, Levi also had a brother named James . . . Little James, they called him. Remember, Simon? He was a sympathizer with our movement.

Simon

(Motioning for Matthew to leave) See you later, Matthew. *(Matthew looks back a couple of times as he exits)*

Barabbas

That guy can call himself lucky, too. I was just a fraction of a second from destroying him! Sure looks like that traitor, Levi. Say . . . look at me. *(Begins laughing and pounding Simon on the back)* Lucky Barabbas! I should have died on that cross! I just wanted to stop by and look at it . . . and thank my lucky stars.

Simon

You *are* fortunate, Barabbas! I hope you realize a very great man died for you!

Barabbas

That's what I hear. A religious fanatic who was very popular with the people. By the way, I've heard, via the prison grapevine, that you were linked up with him in some way. Is that true?

Simon

It's true! I'm one of his apostles. One of the twelve chosen to help him change the world.

Barabbas

Too bad he failed. But, I'll say one thing for him: he knew how to choose a good man when he chose you. I certainly had high hopes for you in the Zealot movement. Say . . . come with me! We can both pick up where our careers were interrupted. I've got some great plans! All those months in isolation were not wasted. Simon, come with me!

Simon

I'm sorry, Barabbas, I could never go back to the old life!

Barabbas

What's happened to you? You gone soft? Don't you remember what happened to your uncle? You watched him die on a cross just like this when you were a little boy. *(Simon cringes)* And, what about your sister, Anna? You haven't forgotten what that platoon of Roman soldiers did to her, have you? Her body, now almost a vegetable . . . and her mind, completely gone!

Simon

(In anguish) I have tried to put all of that out of my mind. Can you imagine the old hatreds against Rome that have tried to raise their ugly heads since I have seen my Captain nailed to a cross? But I have three years of beautiful, good memories, also. Among those good memories, my sister, Anna . . . Jesus healed both her body and mind. A miracle . . . the greatest I've ever seen. And my life . . . Barabbas, I learned the meaning of words like "peace" and "hope" . . . and "love."

Barabbas

Well, that might have been good for the moment, but now he's gone forever! And, you're still young! Together we can do something about these atrocities. *(Points to the cross)* You must want to avenge the death of your friend. *(Puts arm around Simon)* You haven't forgotten what a great team we were, you and I? Jesus was popular with a lot of people . . . his crucifixion is going to give us a lot of sympathizers. It looks like a new day for the Zealots. *(Pleading)* Come with me, Simon!

Simon

Barabbas . . . *(Puts his hands on Barabbas' shoulders, causing Barabbas to have to look him square in the eyes)* Barabbas, I respect you a great deal. I agree with you in many areas. I dislike the oppression and cruelty of Rome. I admire your courage . . . your dedication to your cause. But I cannot go with you. *(Turning away)* I **will** not go with you. When I yielded myself to my new Commander, it was a lifetime vow. He taught me the truth about God. God doesn't hate, he loves. God doesn't want us to try to change the world with hatred, but with love. It works! I've seen it work!

Barabbas

One thing refutes your whole theory . . . look behind you! *(They look up at the cross)* It looks like it works, all right! Where did all that love get him? Crucified! He's dead, Simon! What good is a dead Commander? *(Sarcastically)* Is he going to bark orders to you from the grave? *(He smears his hand in the blood from the cross)* See that, Simon? It's blood . . . Jesus' blood! The only one who will ever benefit from that blood is me! Someday you will come to the realization that he is dead, and the beautiful, but impossible, ideals he fostered died on the cross with him. *(He begins to leave)* Someday you will wise up and realize that what I say is true. When you do, look me up. I can always use another good man with the sica!

Simon

(Watching him leave . . . notices that he still has Barabbas' sica in his hand) The sica . . . *(He calls after Barabbas, but he does not hear)* You forgot something! *(His voice trails off)* Your sica! *(He throws it on the ground)* Jesus . . . Sir . . . I think you would have been proud of me.

I *won!* I won my greatest battle! For these past three days, I have faced the greatest temptation of my life . . . to take up the sica again. But I won! I fought off all of those old hatreds that were pulling at me. I meant it, sir, when I dedicated my life to you. I will be loyal to you though I can no longer hear your voice . . . though I can no longer see you. You are my Commander forever . . . you are my Lord and Captain, and I'll love you in death as I loved you in life.

Anna

(Running breathlessly in, talking very excitedly) Simon, my brother . . . I have been looking everywhere for you. Matthew said I might find you here. He's alive, Simon! Jesus is alive!

Simon

(Calming her) Anna . . . Anna, calm down. What's wrong with you? *(Feels her face for fever)* You're not having a relapse, are you? Too much emotion . . . too much depression . . . too many tears. I'm not surprised!

Anna

I'm feeling fine, Simon. Please believe me . . . it is true! Several of the women have seen him, and when Peter and . . .

Matthew

(Interrupting as he and James the Less run in) Simon . . . Simon . . . Come quickly. He's alive . . . Jesus is alive!

James the Less

(Breathlessly trying to get a word in) He rose from the dead, Simon! Remember how he raised Lazarus? He did

it to himself, too!

Philip
(Coming from side of stage) Simon, I'm glad I found you! It's Jesus . . . he's alive again? Peter and John have already been to the tomb, and it's true . . . his grave is empty!

Simon
(Still in shock) Peter and John found the tomb empty? (Other disciples come in from all sides)

Judas, Not Iscariot
Some of the women saw an angel sitting on the large stone that blocked his tomb.

Simon
What is this? You say he is alive? (Beginning to get excited)

Andrew
Mary Magdalene saw him and even talked to him. She couldn't believe it either; in fact, she at first thought he was the gardener!

Philip
(Breaking in) She says Jesus told her he wanted to meet us — all of us, even Peter, who denied him.

Andrew
I can't find Thomas. Does anyone know where Thomas might be? Now that we have Simon, we've found everyone but Thomas.

Philip
He asked us to meet him . . . we think he might want us

to meet him at the Upper Room. That's where I'm going! He's alive! Can you believe it? He's alive! *(As he exits, others follow very excitedly)*

Judas, Not Iscariot
The grave couldn't hold him! We should have known it!

Anna
(Dancing around in great glee as she leaves; she sings) He's alive, he's alive! He's alive and I'm forgiven! Heaven's gates are open wide. He's alive!

Simon
(Begins weeping . . . calls very loudly in the direction Barabbas has gone) Barabbas! *(With fists clenched)* Barabbas! He's alive! My Commander is alive!

When Old Nick Met Nicodemus

Cast (in order of appearance)

NICK (an old newspaper vendor)
JIM/NICODEMUS (a younger man)
JOSEPH OF ARIMATHEA
SOLDIER I
SOLDIER II
PETER
JOHN
SALOME
MARY
MARY MAGDALENE
EXTRAS

Introduction

We are blessed with a professional actor in our church, who loves to play the part of old men. This play was written with him in mind, but any man with a bit of make-up and whitened hair can win your audience with this warm story of an old man on Easter morning.

The scenery is very simple . . . an old street corner newstand with some magazines and papers hung with clothespins are on one side of the stage and a garden area is on the other side of the platform.

Scene: *On stage left, a street in any major city, U.S.A., with a newspaper stand and a street light. On stage right, a beautiful garden setting. (Stage left setting is contemporary; stage right setting is biblical).*
Time: *Early one Easter morning.*

Nick

(The old man with a cane comes from stage left to the newspaper stand and proceeds to open it, while talking to himself) Sure glad it's not raining today. We've had more than our share already! Maybe it's not so unusual, though. All that talk about April showers bringing flowers . . . maybe it's common that it rains during all of April. Well, sure glad it ain't raining today! *(Looks up sharply, as if looking at street)* Lot more traffic than usual on a Sunday morning . . . it is Sunday, isn't it? *(Takes newspaper, looks at date)* Days all kinda run together. Yeah, Sunday, all right. *(Reads aloud)* FAIR WEATHER FORECAST FOR EASTER! So that's why there's more traffic then usual — it's Easter! *(pauses)* So what? Just another day! *(In contemplation)* Wasn't always that way, though. When my Annie was alive, it was such a special day. *(Chuckles)* Her dyeing eggs and fretting over the baked ham dinner . . . and that tall coconut cake with the little clusters of jelly beans hidden in the coconut. She was always beautiful . . . but at Easter, she had a special glow. *(Pauses with a smile on his face, then the smile turns to sadness)* How I miss her! But I mustn't think about that . . . it hurts too much. I'll just be glad it's not raining, read the morning paper, and get my mind off Annie and all that . . . *(begins reading paper)*

Jim

(Comes from stage left, carrying a biblical costume)

Mor.iing, Nick! Got an extra copy of the *Times*?

Nick
Why, for all get-out, Jim, what brings you out so early on a Sunday morning? *(Speaks while he's getting the newspaper)* Used to seeing you here on a weekday, but not on a Sunday.

Jim
(As he pulls change from his pocket) It's not just Sunday, Nick; it's Easter Sunday! And I'm out so early because I'm on my way to an early service at our church.

Nick
Oh, yeah, I 'most forgot. 'Tis Easter, isn't it?

Jim
Aren't you going to church this morning?

Nick
Who, me? Naw, Jim, I'm afraid not! *(Pauses)* There was a time . . . *(Drifts off into his memories)* My Annie used to go to church every Sunday, and on Easter she would insist that I go with her. We used to get all tuckered up, and my Annie and I went to church. She knew everyone there and always seemed so proud to have me with her. Then we'd go home and have a big holiday dinner. You know . . . *(Startled that he has been talking so much)* Oh, excuse me . . . I kinda got carried away a bit. When a mind is old and lonely, it's easy to get lost in the memories of a happy past. I apologize Jim. I'm sorry.

Jim
You loved Annie so much, why didn't you go to church with her more often?

Nick

That's a question I've asked myself often. Why wasn't I by her side every moment? If I had only known she would suffer that fatal heart attack, I would have done so many things differently. Yes, I would have.

Jim

Why, it's never too late. She'd want you to be in church and preparing yourself to meet her in heaven someday.

Nick

Oh yes, I know that is true. She would want me to be in church and especially on Easter. She always used to say that . . . that . . . let me see, how was that? . . . "Christ's Resurrection was the assurance of her Eternal Life." Yep, that's what she always said.

Jim

And she was right. Why don't you come with me to church this morning? If for no other reason, for Annie's sake!

Nick

Well . . . *(Slowly)* No . . . No I couldn't do that. I don't belong! Now, Annie belonged . . . she was pure and clean and holy. She was as near perfect a wife as a man ever had. But me . . . look at me, Jim! I'm no good! I belong out here on the street with the addicts, and prostitutes, and bums. I ain't worthy to go to God's house, Jim!

Jim

Of course you're not! None of us are. The Bible tells us that all have sinned and come short. Even the Bible characters were sinners, and even those who walked with Jesus failed him. But, what did Jesus do? Did he say, "Get away from me, you failures . . . you sinners!"? No, not at all. He came to them in a resurrected body, forgave them, and loved them. We are doing a play in church that kind of talks about how they failed the Lord.

Nick

A play in church?

Jim

Yes, a drama that helps us understand a bit of the joy and excitement of the first Easter. *(Holds up the costume)* I'm playing the part of a man named Nicodemus.

Nick

(Getting excited) Nicodemus? Did you know that is my full name? I've never liked it, so I just use Nick. But my mother always told me it was a nice Bible name. Come to think of it, I don't even know who Nicodemus *was* in the Bible.

Jim

Well, then, you must come and see this play and learn more about your namesake! You see, I play the part of Nicodemus, and I wear this costume. It's the costume of a wealthy man, because Nicodemus was a very wealthy and important man. He was a member of the high court for Israel. Let me tell you about our play. Pretend you are in a beautiful garden at sunrise that very first Easter . . . there you will see Nicodemus — that's me — waiting for a friend to come.

(Old Nick freezes; the lights fade to dim on the newsstand and brighten on the garden portion of the set. Jim proceeds to assume the role of Nicodemus for the play)

Nicodemus

He's not here yet! *(Looking around)* But then, perhaps I am a bit early. It's so quiet this morning . . . like the quiet after a great storm. Eerie and quiet! What a stormy week it has been! *(Gesturing across center stage)* Jersualem is now quiet after the great holiday week. No more singing or dancing in the streets. Even the loudest of revelers are sleeping off a drunken hangover! And over there *(Gesturing to stage right),* Golgotha's Hill, with her three empty crosses silhouetting the sunrise, is also strangely quiet. Oh, the sounds that emanated from that hill this week! Sounds of steel against steel as hammers drove nails . . . sounds of women weeping and crowds jeering . . . and a pleading voice from the cross, begging, "Father, forgive them, for they know not what they do!" *(Joseph slips up unnoticed)* And now . . . it is all so strangely quiet!

Joseph of Arimathea

Yes, it is quiet *(Nicodemus is startled at first)* except for the cackling of those vultures over on Calvary at the town garbage heap, fighting over the bodies of the two thieves who were crucified with Jesus.

Nicodemus

What a wonderful thing you have done, Joseph, giving Jesus your newly carved tomb!

Joseph of Arimathea

It was the least I could do. I feel as though I failed him so much, while he was alive.

Nicodemus

Now don't start that again! You only did what you thought was best. You were sure that being a secret disciple could be of more help to his cause than openly confessing him.

Joseph of Arimathea
No, that's not the only reason I remained a secret disciple. I was a coward! I was fearful for my position. I was a failure to him when he needed me so desperately!

Nicodemus
What do you mean? You stood with me, in support of Jesus in the meeting of the Sanhedrin!

Joseph of Arimathea
Yes, but it was too late! Too late! For three days I have wept out in repentance for my failure. But it is too late!

Nicodemus
(Taking Joseph by the shoulder) Joseph, I have something I want to share with you. Something I have just discovered in the Scripture. I don't need to remind you how we have had faith in the great prophets of our people . . . how they had promised the dawning of a better day. In spite of all the present evils and injustices, we looked to a day when these should be done away with . . . a time when justice should flow down like waters, and righteousness as a mighty stream. A day when men would beat their swords into plowshares and learn war no more. Joseph, you recall how we studied all the prophecies and how all of them pointed to Jesus as our Messiah. Do you remember how excited we were?

Joseph of Arimathea
Yes, but now what? He's dead!

Nicodemus

Since Friday, I have searched the Scriptures. Joseph, everything that has happened this week has been prophesied! When I read the book of the Prophet Isaiah, it was just like reading an account of what happened to Jesus this week. It was all foretold, Joseph . . . his death, his denial, his betrayal . . . and, Joseph, if I read the Scripture right, your giving Jesus your new tomb is foretold. In Isaiah it reads, "he made his grave with the rich." Do you know what this means? Your begging for his body so that it would not be thrown on the garbage heap . . . your taking that body to your own tomb in this garden . . . it is all in fulfillment of prophecy!

Joseph of Arimathea

Is that written there, Nicodemus? That's exciting! But, what does it all mean? So he fulfilled all of our dreams and the scriptural prophecies. . . he's dead now! What good can come of all this?

Nicodemus

Let's have faith, and not question. I am learning that as it happens and as we compare it to prophecy, there is a perfect correlation. *(He pauses, then smiles)* Look at us . . . we have not even greeted each other yet! Good morning, friend Joseph!

Joseph of Arimathea

And good morning to you.

Nicodemus

I see you have brought the spices and linens for a proper burial.

Joseph of Arimathea
Yes, some of the women believers have offered to meet us here to give him a decent embalming. It was so late on the evening of the Sabbath that we could not give him proper preparation for the tomb.

Nicodemus
What a beautiful thing you have done in giving him your tomb. And it is fulfillment of prophecy, I am sure.

(Two very excited soldiers run in, interrupting this last line)

Soldier I
Joseph, how glad we are to see you!

Soldier II
(Gesturing greatly) Just rolled back, . . . just rolled, and rolled, and rolled, and rolled!

Joseph of Arimathea
What is all of this about? Have you two been drinking?

Soldier I
All of the other soldiers of the guard have fled. They have all gone back to the barracks, or to Herod, or to Pilate, or somewhere.

Soldier II
(Gesturing excitedly) Yeah, they all fled. They were scared! They all ran . . . they all fled . . . *(Gestures)*

Nicodemus
You *have* been drinking, haven't you?

Soldier I

No sir, not a drop!

Soldier II

No sir, no sir, no sir! We are stone sober! But I sure could use a drink. Yes sir, yes sir, I sure could!

Soldier I

Let me start at the beginning . . . we were just sitting around the campfire, don't you see? Some of us were sleeping *(Soldier II demonstrates);* others of us were visiting and laughing; when, all of a sudden, a great light appeared!

Soldier II

(Getting very excited) I'll say . . . a powerful light, brighter than a thousand candles. No, brighter than 10,000 candles. No, it was brighter than a hundred thousand candles! No, it was brighter than . . .

Soldier I

(Interrupting) And then an angel appeared to us . . . with eyes that were flaming like coals of fire.

Soldier II

Yes, yes, yes, yes . . . two giant fireballs . . . just staring at us. Like huge coals of fire that were spitting out sparks. Huge fireballs *(he shudders)* . . . can you even imagine these balls of fire? . . .

Soldier I

(Interrupting again) And the angel never said a word. And those who were asleep just slept on, and those of us who were awake literally passed out with fear!

Soldier II

(Very excited) Just passed right out! I was so afraid of those two fireballs staring at me, I just passed right out! I was just out like everyone else . . . just like this *(falls down)* Konk! I was just out!

Soldier I

(Interrupting again) When I came to, I looked up, and the stone started rolling. The angel was rolling it all by himself . . . that giant stone! By this time, some of the others were awake and woke up those who were asleep. And when they saw that giant stone rolling and the bright light that came from inside the tomb, they started running.

Soldier II

Yeah, they all started running . . . they just fled. But not I! No sir, I did not run! I just went konk, and passed out again. That giant stone, she was just a rollin' and a rollin' and a rollin'!

Soldier I

(Interrupting) And Jesus simply sat up and folded the linen garment and walked out!

Soldier II

Now, I didn't see that . . . I was still konked out from that stone a rollin'

Soldier I

It was incredible! I have never been so afraid!

Soldier II

Yeah, my knees are still a knockin' and a knockin' and a knockin'.

Nicodemus

You realize, don't you, that as members of the Sanhedrin, we must report you for drinking on the job? Now, report back to your barracks immediately.

Soldier I

(As they begin to depart) But sir, we were not drinking! Please believe me!

Soldier II

No sir, no sir, no sir! But I need a good strong drink now, yes sir, yes sir!

(Peter and John run onto stage from s .ge right; this frightens the soldiers even more)

Peter

(Excitedly; breathlessly) Mary Magdalene was right . . . the tomb is empty!

John

Mary came early. She said she saw him, and talked to him. Jesus is alive again! It's a miracle, like he did to Lazarus!

(Women run down aisle while they are talking)

Salome

He's gone! The stone is rolled back, and two angels were sitting on the marble slab!

Mary

It's true! Unbelievable, but true!

Mary Magdalene

(Shouting) He's alive, everybody! I saw him! I talked to him! Believe me, he's alive! *(Background music starts)*

Nicodemus

Of course! Remember, he said, "If you destroy this Temple, after three days I will raise it up." This must have been what he meant.

Joseph of Arimathea

And I recall him saying, "As Jonah was three days and three nights in the belly of the whale, so must the Son of man be three days and nights in the earth." He must have meant in a tomb!

Peter

That's right! I remember him saying that, also.

(Music keeps increasing in volume)

Mary Magdalene

All I know is, he's alive! I talked to him! Jesus is alive!

(Others of choir run in shouting, "He's alive!" as choir begins to sing an Easter song of victory such as, "Christ the Lord is Risen Today")

(After song, cast in the garden scene freezes, lights in garden scene fade; and lights become brighter in newstand scene. Nicodemus walks out of garden scene back into newstand scene; once again assuming the role of Jim and removing his robe)

Nick

(Kind of misty-eyed) That's a beautiful story, Jim. Really beautiful! I'm named after a pretty good guy, ain't I? You say you're going to be performing this play at church this morning?

Jim

(While taking off robe) We sure are, and I got to get going, or I'm going to be late. Guess I got a bit carried away telling you about it!

Nick

Do you suppose . . . (Pauses) Perhaps . . . Well, do you think . . . I know it would make my Annie happy . . . if . . .

Jim

Do you want to go with me?

Nick

Do you suppose they'd let the likes of me in?

Jim

Why, of course they would! They'd love to have you! *(Nick begins speedily closing up his newspaper stand)* And, after church, why not come to our house and have dinner with us? Grace was putting the ham on to bake when I left. She's bringing the children to the later service.

Nick

Will she have some dyed eggs, too?

Jim

(As they begin walking out on stage left) She sure does! And I saw the tallest coconut cake you ever saw, and it

had little nests of colored jellybeans hidden in the coconut . . .

(As the two walk off, the lights come up in the garden area, and the biblical cast sings a reprise of their song as a finale.)

www.ingramcontent.com/pod-product-compliance
Lightning Source LLC
Chambersburg PA
CBHW060042040426
42331CB00032B/2245